T0045432

Using Your Five Senses

Andrew Collins

Contents

Five Senses

Pretend you are sitting by a campfire. What can you see and feel? You can see different colors in the flames. If you're sitting close, you can feel the warmth of the fire. You probably smell smoke and may hear the fire crackling. If you're lucky, you may even get to taste toasted marshmallows.

How did you know the fire was smokey, warm, and bright? Your body has five sense organs—the eyes, ears, nose, tongue, and skin. Your sense organs gather information and send it to your brain. Then your brain lets you know what you are seeing, hearing, smelling, tasting, and feeling.

Your sense organs gather information to help your brain make sense of your world.

3

Of all your senses, you probably use your sense of sight the most. More than two-thirds of the information processed in your brain comes in through your eyes. Your eyes tell you about an object's shape and color. They also tell you how big an object is and whether it's near or far.

How Do We See?

Did you know seeing happens in your brain, not in your eyes? Here's how it works.

Light comes into your eyes through your **pupil**, the dark center of your eye. After the light goes through your pupil, it travels through the **lens** in the front of your eye. The lens focuses the light into a sharp image on the **retina** in the back of your eye.

The pupil gets smaller in bright light and larger in dim light.

4

The retina changes information about the light into signals your brain can understand. Your brain receives the signals and interprets them—all in the blink of an eye!

The Eye

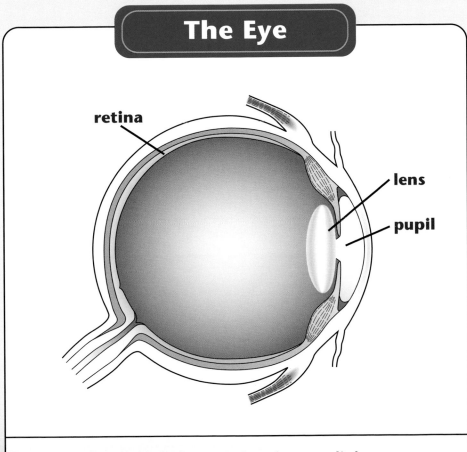

retina

lens

pupil

lens	the part of the eye that focuses light
pupil	an opening in the eye that lets in light
retina	the part of the eye where light is changed into signals the brain can understand

The World of Sight

Your eyes let you see many things. But how do human eyes compare to eyes in the animal kingdom?

Giant Squid A giant squid has only one eye. But its eye is about the size of your head! The squid uses its large eye to see in the deep dark ocean waters where it lives.

Tarsier A tarsier is a small animal that lives in the rain forest. It has really large eyes that help it see well in the dim light in the forest.

Eagle An eagle can see eight times better than humans can. Eagles have the best vision in the animal kingdom. They are great hunters.

Tarsier

Eagle

Try This!

Roll a piece of paper into a tube. Hold the tube up to your left eye. Hold your right hand up next to the tube. Now look straight ahead. What do you see?

Do you really have a hole in your hand? No! But each of your eyes sent a slightly different image to your brain. When your brain combined the two images into one, it got confused. Your brain told you there was a hole in your hand when there really wasn't!

7

Hearing

Hearing affects our lives in many ways. Your favorite song might cheer you up. A friend's joke might make you laugh. Hearing can also help keep you safe. Some sounds warn you of possible danger. You might hear a car coming before you see it.

How Do We Hear?

Your ears are the sense organs that gather sound information. Like seeing, hearing actually happens in your brain. Here's how it works.

Sounds enter your outer ear. Your outer ear includes the parts you can see on the outside of your head and the **ear canal**.

Sounds then move down the ear canal to the middle ear. The sounds bounce off the **eardrum**, making it vibrate, or move quickly back and forth. These vibrations then move to the inner ear.

In the inner ear, the **cochlea** changes the sound vibrations into signals the brain can understand. These signals are sent to your brain. Your brain then makes sense of what you are hearing.

The Ear

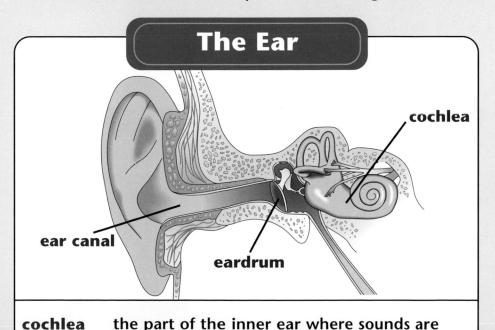

cochlea

ear canal

eardrum

cochlea	the part of the inner ear where sounds are changed into signals the brain can understand
ear canal	the part of the outer ear that leads to the eardrum
eardrum	a thin, flexible part of the middle ear that vibrates when sounds bounce off it

The World of Hearing

Our ears do an amazing job. But many animals hear much better than we do.

Bat A bat uses its hearing to find its food. It sends out sounds that bounce off things in its path. The sounds then bounce back to the bat, telling it where the flying insects are.

Owl Many owls hunt at night. They use their excellent hearing to help them catch food.

Fox Foxes have large ears that help them hear the sounds of small animals.

Fox

Owl

Have a friend stand across the room and whisper to you. Listen carefully. Now cup your ears with your hands. Have your friend whisper again. Your friend probably sounded louder the second time. Why is that? When you cup your ears, you help your ears catch more sound waves, which made the whisper sound louder.

Smell

Each day your sense of smell affects you. The smell of rotten food keeps you from eating it. The smell of smoke can warn people of danger. And the smell of freshly baked cookies can make people very hungry.

How Do We Smell?

A person with a good sense of smell can recognize as many as 10,000 different odors. When you smell an odor, your nose gathers information and sends that information to your brain. Here's how it works.

As you breathe, air enters your two **nostrils**. As this air travels to your lungs, it passes through your **nasal cavity**. In the nasal cavity, odors pass special cells at the top of your nose. These cells collect information about the odors.

Nerves then send this information to your brain. In an instant, your brain receives the information and figures out what you are smelling.

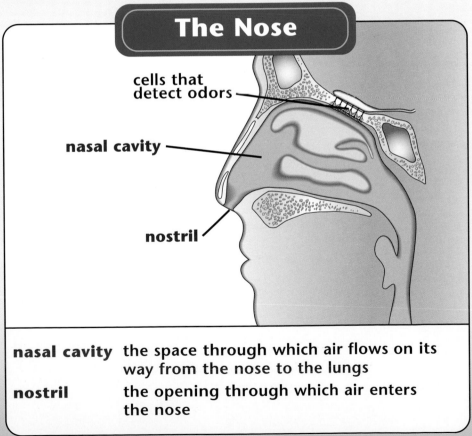

The Nose

cells that detect odors

nasal cavity

nostril

nasal cavity	the space through which air flows on its way from the nose to the lungs
nostril	the opening through which air enters the nose

The World of Smell

Almost all the animals in the world have a better sense of smell than people do. Some animals have different ways of smelling.

Bloodhound A bloodhound's sense of smell is hundreds of times better than a human's. Police have used these dogs to find lost children and catch criminals.

Pig A pig can use its sense of smell to find food under the ground.

Snake A snake smells through its nostrils. But it also senses odors by flicking its tongue in and out of its mouth.

Snake

Bloodhound

Try This!

Next time you go to a flower shop, notice the odors you smell when you first walk in. After five minutes, decide if you can still smell those odors. You probably can't. What has happened? You are experiencing odor fatigue. Odor fatigue happens when you've been exposed to the same smell for more than a few minutes. At that point, your nose stops sending smell signals to your brain.

15

Taste

Your sense of taste helps protect you from eating spoiled or poisonous foods. It helps you choose foods that can keep you healthy. And, of course, your sense of taste makes eating fun.

How Do We Taste?

When you taste something, nerves on your tongue sense food and send taste messages to your brain. Here's how it works.

Taste begins on your tongue. Your tongue is covered with **taste buds**. Most people have about 10,000 taste buds. Taste buds can sense four basic tastes: sweet, sour, bitter, and salty.

Each taste bud has a small opening. Inside each opening arc cells that detect taste when tiny bits of food move across the opening. Information about the food is changed into signals.

These signals are sent to your brain. At the same time information about the food's smell is also sent to your brain. Your brain receives these signals and identifies what you are tasting.

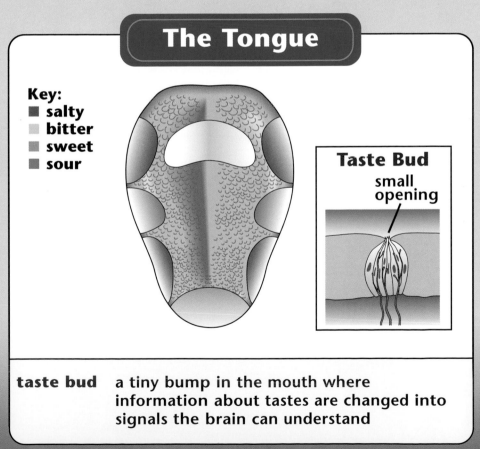

The Tongue

Key:
- ◼ salty
- ◻ bitter
- ◼ sweet
- ◼ sour

Taste Bud

small opening

taste bud	a tiny bump in the mouth where information about tastes are changed into signals the brain can understand

The World of Taste

Many animals have more taste buds than people. Let's see how taste buds are used in the animal kingdom.

Catfish A catfish may have the most taste buds of all—175,000! Most of them are on the outside of the catfish's body and on its feelers. The taste buds help the fish identify food as it swims.

Fly Flies have their taste buds on their feet. Next time you see a fly walking on your plate, remember it is actually tasting your food with its feet!

Catfish

Fly

How important is your nose when you're tasting food? Try this with a friend. Cut an apple, pear, and raw potato into pieces of the same size. Blindfold your friend. Have your friend hold his or her nose tightly closed. Invite your friend to taste each food, one at a time. Could your friend tell which food was which?

Your friend probably couldn't tell which taste was the apple, the pear, or the potato. Without the help of your sense of smell, it is hard to recognize the taste of food.

Touch

Your skin is one giant sense organ. It is by far the largest sense organ you have. Your sense of touch allows you to feel pain, heat, cold, and pressure. It tells you when to move away from a hot stove or when to put on warmer clothes. Your sense of touch also lets you enjoy a friend's hug or the feel of your dog's fur.

How Do We Feel?

Your skin gathers information about how things feel. Your nerves send this information to your brain. Here's how it works.

There are thousands of tiny **nerve endings** in your skin. These nerve endings are scattered all over your body. There are several different kinds of nerve endings. Some sense pressure. Others sense hot and cold temperatures. Still others sense pain.

Every time you touch something, signals are sent to your brain. Your brain then identifies the touch and tells you what you are feeling.

Skin

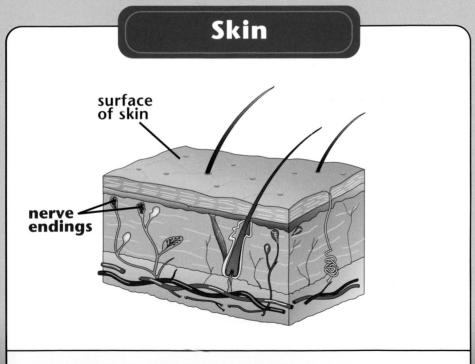

surface
of skin

nerve
endings

nerve endings cells in the skin that change information about pressure, pain, and temperature into signals the brain can understand

The World of Touch

Animals use touch in many of the same ways we do. They use touch to tell if their food is too hot or too cold. Some use touch to communicate.

Cat A cat's whiskers are about as wide as the cat's body. At the base of their whiskers, cats have very sensitive nerve endings. They can feel their whiskers bending backwards. This tells them that the space they are entering may be too small for them.

Mole Moles use their sense of touch to find food underground.

Cat

Mole

Try This!

Which parts of your body are very sensitive to temperature? Put your elbow, toe, and finger in a bowl of warm water. Which part feels the warmest?

Your toe will feel the warmest, your elbow the coolest. That's because there are more nerve endings that are sensitive to temperature in your toe than in your elbow.

23

Index